My name is

_____

This is my book.

Will you please read it to me?

Thank you.

Grammy's Superhero LLC, Royersford, PA
Feather's Santa Train Surprise!
Text, Illustration & Book design copyright @ 2019 by Grammy's Superhero LLC
www.grammyssuperhero.com

Text by Wendy Kerr Sherid
Photography, llustration and design by Janet M. Jones
Creativity by Callen Bram Sheridan
Editing by Sharleen Sensenig

All rights reserved, including the right of reproduction in whole or in part in any form.

Manufactured in the United States of America

ISBN:9781695638082

**Photos enhanced by PRISMA® LABS app
Building the future of photo and video editing**

FEATHER'S SANTA TRAIN SURPRISE!

WRITTEN BY
WENDY KERR SHERID
ILLUSTRATED BY
JANET M. JONES

Dedication:

This book is dedicated to the Chester County Puppy Club, with a special thank you to the wonderful Puppy Raisers who shared their day for a ride on the Strasburg Railroad Steam Train, Strasburg, PA with Callen, Feather and I.

Although in the book we depict a wintery, snowy day, in reality, it was a cold, rainy and miserable afternoon; The kind of day where you'd rather curl up on the sofa with a cup of hot chocolate.

But they came out willingly to help their pups learn about the sights, sounds and feel of train travel, and to help me out by being enthusiastic models in Feather's Santa Train Surprise.

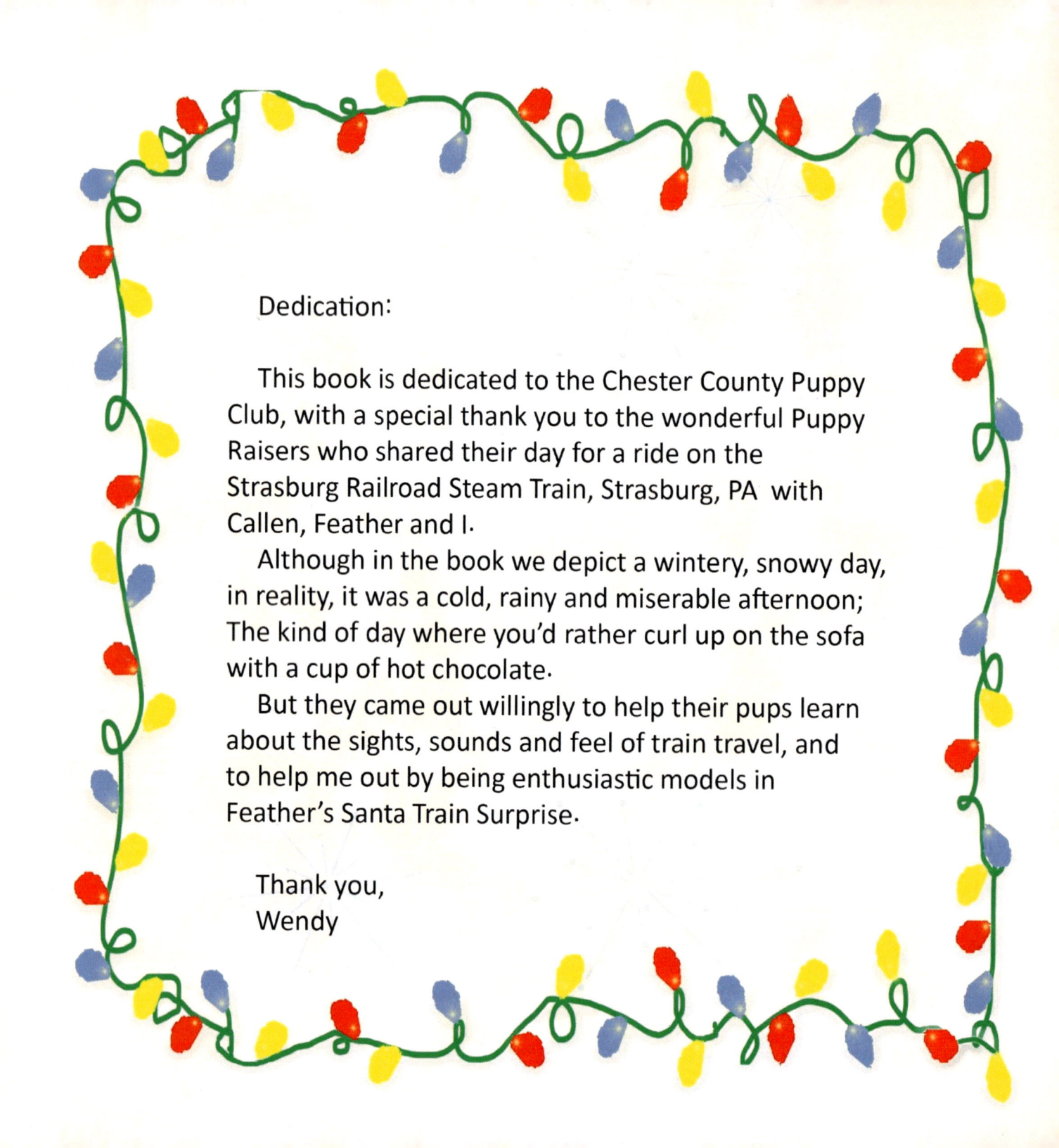

Thank you,
Wendy

Winter is in the air and Christmas is just a few weeks away. A light snow has blanketed the town where Grammy lives with her Seeing Eye® dog, Feather. Grammy's grandson, Callen, and his dad, are picking Grammy and Feather up for a special trip on the Strasburg Railroad Santa Train. Grammy has a few surprises in store for both Callen and Feather!

Before they leave for the train, Grammy must feed and 'park' Feather.
Park is the word Grammy uses to tell Feather it is time to go outside and go to the bathroom.

Feather has a schedule of times to go out. She sniffs the ground and circles around Grammy until she finds just the right spot.

After Feather parks, Grammy can't resist playing with her in the newly fallen snow.

She gets into the fun by throwing snowballs into the air for Feather to catch.

When Callen and his dad arrive, Callen runs over to Grammy. Grammy knows fun time is over. She needs to switch Feather to work time by putting on her harness.

Grammy calls Feather over to the patio to get ready. First, she puts the harness over Feather's head. Next, Grammy leans down to put the leather strap under Feather's belly and through the strap that goes around her body. Finally, she hooks the leash on Feather's collar.

Feather is ready to guide Grammy around safely. Feather and Grammy climb into the SUV with Callen and his dad for the long drive to the train station.

When they arrive at the station, Grammy, Feather and Callen spot some puppies and their puppy raisers near the ticket booth.

Grammy and Callen
go to the window to buy
their tickets.
Then Grammy tells Callen to
turn around for his first
surprise.

Callen spots Cormac and runs over to his side. Cormac is the new friend Callen made during "Feather's Playground Adventure."

The conductor tells Grammy and the children they can wait by the wood stove in the warm train station. The Santa Train will be here in 15 minutes.

When they walk into the station, Seeing Eye® puppies are everywhere, waiting patiently by the warm wood stove. "Surprise!" says Grammy, "The puppies and their raisers will be riding the Santa Train with us!"

"Hooray!" yell Callen and Cormac as the conductor announces, "HERE COMES THE SANTA TRAIN!"

The puppies and their raisers line up to board a special car reserved just for them. Feather and the puppies are very excited to see what is on board the train.

Once on the train, Callen and his dad settle into a seat across from Cormac and his mom.

Feather settles in quietly with Grammy, just like she learned a long time ago in puppy training.

Before the ride begins, Grammy gives Callen and Cormac a box of Seeing Eye approved bones, festively decorated for Christmas, to hand out to the curious puppies.

What better way to divert the puppies attention from the moving train than to give each one a bone to chew and play with.

As the puppies begin to relax with their treats, Callen tells Cormac how the puppies are here to learn that traveling on trains is a good thing and can be fun.

For the puppies, this is a new experience. The feel of the train swishing back and forth and the 'clackety clack' sound of the wheels on the track are all very strange to them.

The train ride has just begun when guess who stops by? It's Santa Clause! Making a special visit to see whether everyone on board has been naughty or nice!

Perdy whispers in Santa's ear. She wants to assure him that she is trying her best to be on the 'Nice' list.

After Santa visits with the puppies and the children, the jolly elf leaves the train car with a festive "Ho, Ho, Ho!"

As the train claps along the rails, the puppies begin to settle down. They are taking their cues from Feather, who has been lying quietly under Grammy's seat since the start of the ride.

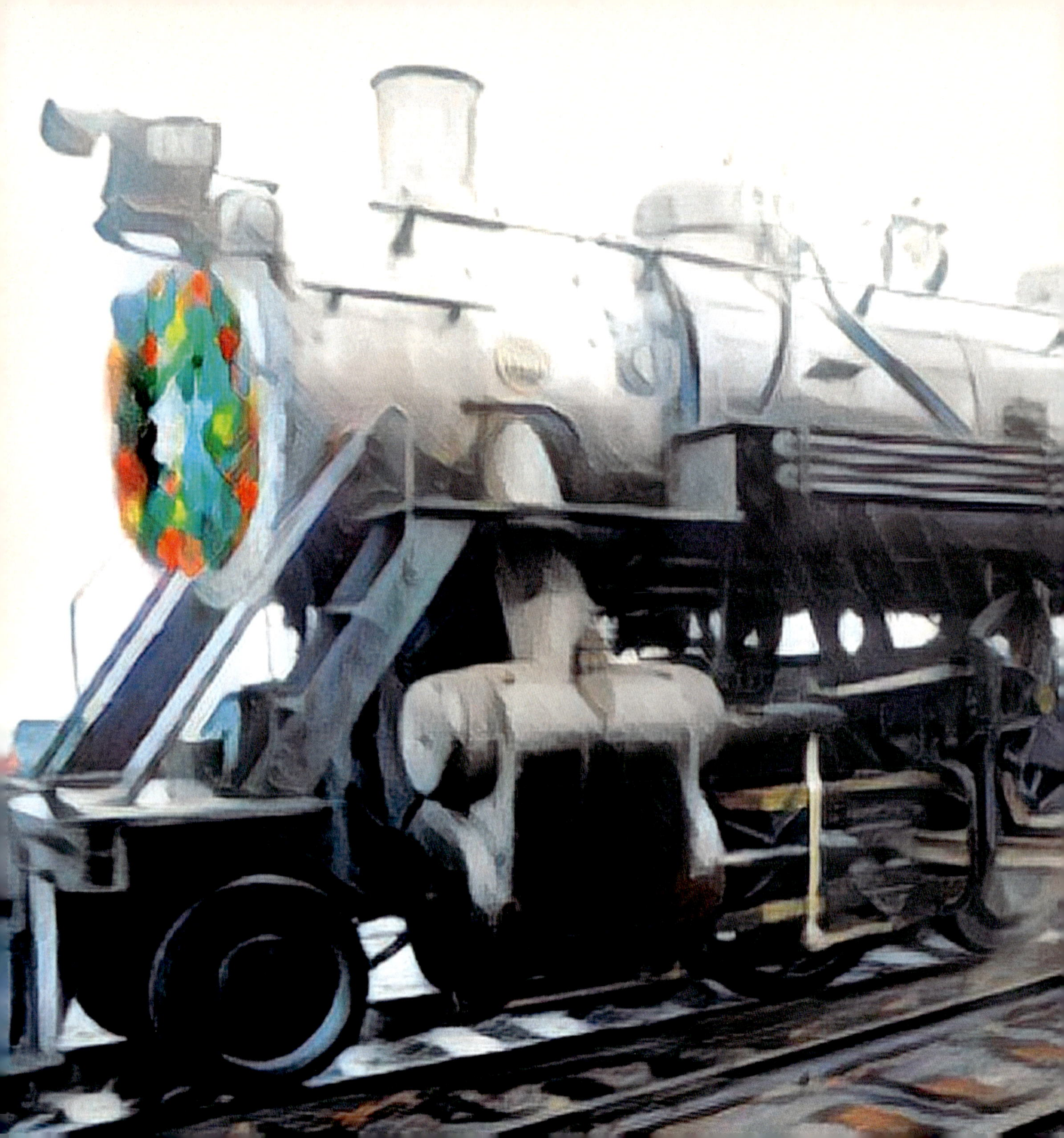

The conductor announces the train has come to the end of the line and they must switch the engine position.

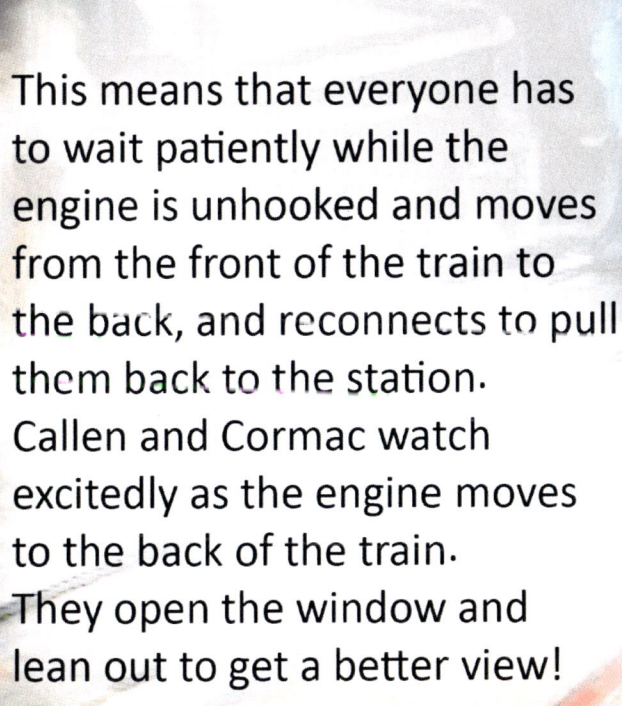

This means that everyone has to wait patiently while the engine is unhooked and moves from the front of the train to the back, and reconnects to pull them back to the station. Callen and Cormac watch excitedly as the engine moves to the back of the train. They open the window and lean out to get a better view!

On the way back to the station, Callen and Cormac watch the puppies to see if they can tell how each puppy is feeling about the train ride.

Zeke is nosy and playful with Cormac. Rory is calm and keeps a close eye on her raiser. Heston is alert but still a bit leery of this whole experience.

Little Perdy snuggles in for a nap as Rory settles down to chew on her Christmas bone. Callen smiles knowing these puppies will grow-up to be someone's Superhero like Feather.

Finally, the train arrives back at the station. Feather helps Grammy find the exit and guides her safely down the steps. "Good girl!" says Grammy. Feather is always happy when Grammy shows her appreciation.
What a wonderful experience this has been for the puppies in training.

The Santa Train ride is over and everyone heads home. The puppies learned a new skill, Callen and Cormac got to see each other again, and Grammy and Feather enjoyed the day and wondered who will earn their harness.
It takes a lot of skills and dedication to be a Seeing Eye®dog!

THE END

Let's talk about this book ....

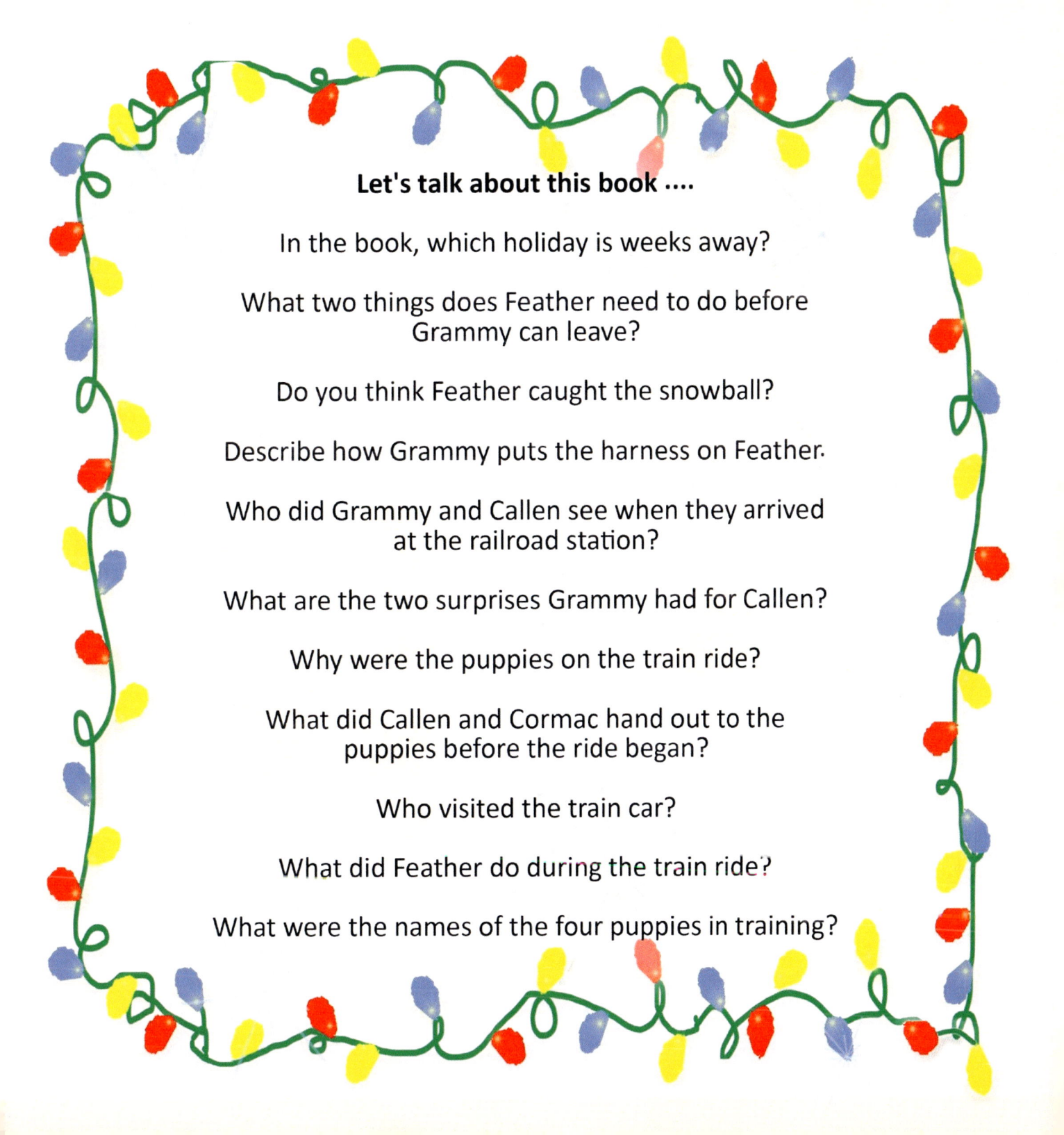

In the book, which holiday is weeks away?

What two things does Feather need to do before Grammy can leave?

Do you think Feather caught the snowball?

Describe how Grammy puts the harness on Feather.

Who did Grammy and Callen see when they arrived at the railroad station?

What are the two surprises Grammy had for Callen?

Why were the puppies on the train ride?

What did Callen and Cormac hand out to the puppies before the ride began?

Who visited the train car?

What did Feather do during the train ride?

What were the names of the four puppies in training?

This is the story of how The Seeing Eye was started

Two years before meeting Morris Frank, Dorothy Harrison Eustis had written a magazine article about training dogs to guide people who are blind or visually impaired – an idea most people at the time thought impossible.

Morris, who was blind, asked Dorothy to train a dog to guide him. He promised that if she trained a dog for him, he would open a school to provide guide dogs to others who needed them.

The first Seeing Eye® dog was a female German shepherd named Kiss. Morris renamed her Buddy.

The two would visit cities across the United States, proving it really was possible for a blind person to be guided by a dog.

On January 29, 1929, Morris and Dorothy founded The Seeing Eye. Ninety years later, the Seeing Eye continues to breed, raise, and train Seeing Eye® dogs. People who are blind come from across the United States and Canada to the school's campus in Morristown, New Jersey, to learn how to work with and care for these amazing animals.

If you would like to know more about The Seeing Eye, visit their website at www.SeeingEye.org.

Watch for these titles, coming soon in the

Grammy's Superheroes Series

Feather Goes to School

Feather Visits Puppy Training

Feather, My Superhero

What's Next for Grammy

Ms. Bee and Me

Coming Home with Ms. Bee

Also by Wendy Kerr Sherid

Feather's Playground Adventure

Nap Time with Feather

Find us at www.grammyssuperhero.com

Made in the
USA
Columbia, SC